JONATHAN PARSONS

JAMES HOCKEY GALLERY

Acknowledgements

I would like to extend my thanks to Christine Kapteijn, without whose tireless work this exhibition and catalogue would not have come into being; Richard Salmon, for his enthusiasm and his generous co-operation and assistance; Ray Carpenter for the design and production of this book; Tanya Harrod for splendidly evincing the interconnectedness of things; my family and wonderful friends for their love and support, particularly during sad and difficult times. Many thanks to Vera Harding of George Tutill Ltd for her care and attention to detail in overseeing the production of all my flag works, and to Peter Johnson of Stephenson Design Plastics for the construction of the acrylic cases which house the dissected maps. Special thanks go to Joan Key, Peter Cross, Jean-Paul Martinon and Paul Heber-Percy who provided me with early opportunities to exhibit and to the lenders who have made important works available for each venue. I also particularly wish to thank James Moores, Alexander Sainsbury, Charles Cormick, Colin Heber-Percy, Neil Tennant, and Penny Johnson at the Government Art Collection. I would finally like to express my deepest gratitude to my wife, Yolaine, who is a constant source of encouragement, understanding and inspiration.

Jonathan Parsons

FRONT COVER
Commune 1998 (detail)
31 sewn polyester flags with wall mounted flagstaffs

PAGE I
Memento 1996
Embossed plastic card, edition of ninety-nine
size 'a': 54 x 86 mm (2⅛ x 3⅜ in)

709·2 PAR

4

BELIEVE HALF YOU SEE
AND NOTHING YOU HEAR

SYSTEM + STRUCTURE

Introduction

In his book *Visual Explanations* Edward Tufte reminds us that the US space shuttle *Challenger* burst into flames on 28 January 1986 because of two rubber sealant rings. They failed due to cold weather. Tufte illustrates some of the thirteen charts urgently faxed to the launch station by the rocket's engineers demonstrating the errant behaviour of the sealant rings at low temperature. But, Tufte concludes, these were ignored because of 'a scandalous discrepancy between the intellectual tasks at hand and the images created to serve these tasks'.[1] The charts looked inconsequential. They were too crude and quotidian, and as a result the *Challenger* crew perished. Tufte's analysis of how information is conveyed through charts, grids, maps, pictographs and carved inscriptions makes vivid our constant struggle with what he calls 'Flatland' – a term he borrows from Edwin Abbot's famous fantasy of a two dimensional world. Tufte writes with wonder – and at times with horror – about the implications of his subject. How is it possible meaningfully to translate information into two dimensions in a fashion that conveys the messy convergence of time, place and materials?

The questions raised by Tufte translate easily to the fine arts. But in the late nineteenth century the analysis of high art abandoned its technical and philosophical curiosity in favour of a discipline called 'art history', dominated by a diachronic trudge from artist to artist, from school to school. This connoisseurly activity, governed consciously or unconsciously by the art market, assessed art according to some measure of progress – from Giotto outstripping Cimabue in what Berenson called 'tactile values' to the ambitiousness of 'American type painting' identified by Clement Greenberg. Few artists – the subjects of the discipline – were interested in this chronological model even if it neatly buttressed the idea of a constantly renewed avant-garde. From the beginnings of Western art and on into the twentieth century artists have valued research – research into the work of earlier artists and into procedures

1 Edward Tufte, *Visual Explanations: Images and Quantities, Evidence and Narrative*, Graphics Press, 1997, p.45.

5

which make sense of the work of representation. Even Vasari, who is usually blamed for an evolutionary approach, put a host of political, economic and socio-psychological ideas into his *Lives of the Artists* and prefaced the whole thing with a brilliant set of technical treatises.[2]

The term 'procedure', with its implication of planning and controlled facture, precisely suggests the spirit of investigation which informs the limpid art of Jonathan Parsons. His particular procedures result from contemporary concerns which can be crudely summarised under two headings. Firstly, why make art at all in such a 'full' world? Secondly, how is it possible to come to terms with the worn rhetoric of the avant-garde in which a work of art is measured by its progressive uniqueness?[3] Until recently artists have had to deal with these problems largely unaided; for evidence we have the conceptual 'art of refusal' of the 1960s and early 1970s, rediscovered in the recent exhibition *Live in Your Head*.[4] But then only in the last twenty years have art history and art criticism caught up with the study of literature, anthropology and history and begun to pose the big questions: what is visual art? what is its relation to power? to perception? to tradition?[5]

These two concerns – why make and on what terms – are connected. One way of resolving the problem of a full world, as Parsons demonstrates so eloquently, is to copy, to remake, to reconstitute what already exists. And in effect this challenges the shibboleth of originality which haunts the idea of the avant-garde. With the exception of his grid paintings Parsons always works from a semiotically powerful source, from something already made. This might be an existing object, like a map, which he manipulates. Or it might be something more ephemeral like a mark or a graffito which he records photographically. Each demands to be remade differently and he looks for 'the most appropriate technique' to produce a 'display' of a given source. Painting might be one medium, but equally so might embroidery or gold tooling or computer graphics. His willingness to employ craft media seems peculiarly contemporary. His cautious use of the word display, on the other hand, takes us back a long way – to Book X of *The Republic* in which Plato argues that the depiction of an object merely represents at two removes what was made by God or manufactured by an artisan. For Plato the artist was a charlatan, never penetrating beneath the superficial appearance of anything. This is a claim that still animates debates about reality and appearance. Parsons responds investigatively to this Platonic negativity. His practice works profoundly hard to alert the viewer to the artificiality of visual representation – by re-presenting or disclosing images and by employing intricate modes of production.

A starting point for an understanding of Parsons' work might be his oil painting *From Nature*. The title is less ironic than it seems. Four calligraphic

2 See Michael Baxendall, *Doing Justice to Vasari*, Times Literary Supplement, 1 February 1980, p.111.

3 For a pioneering critique see Rosalind Krauss, *The Originality of the Avant-Garde & Other Modernist Myths*, MIT, 1985.

4 Whitechapel Art Gallery, *Live in Your Head: Concept and Experiment in Britain 1965–75*, London 2000.

5 Questions posed by Norman Bryson in *Vision and Painting: The Logic of the Gaze*, Macmillan, 1983, p.xi.

Kiss 1994
Chalk on black paper
460 x 495 mm (18¼ x 19½ in)

Kunstwerke

Where Art Exists 1996
Watercolour on paper
diptych, each panel 355 x 1104 mm (14 x 43½ in)

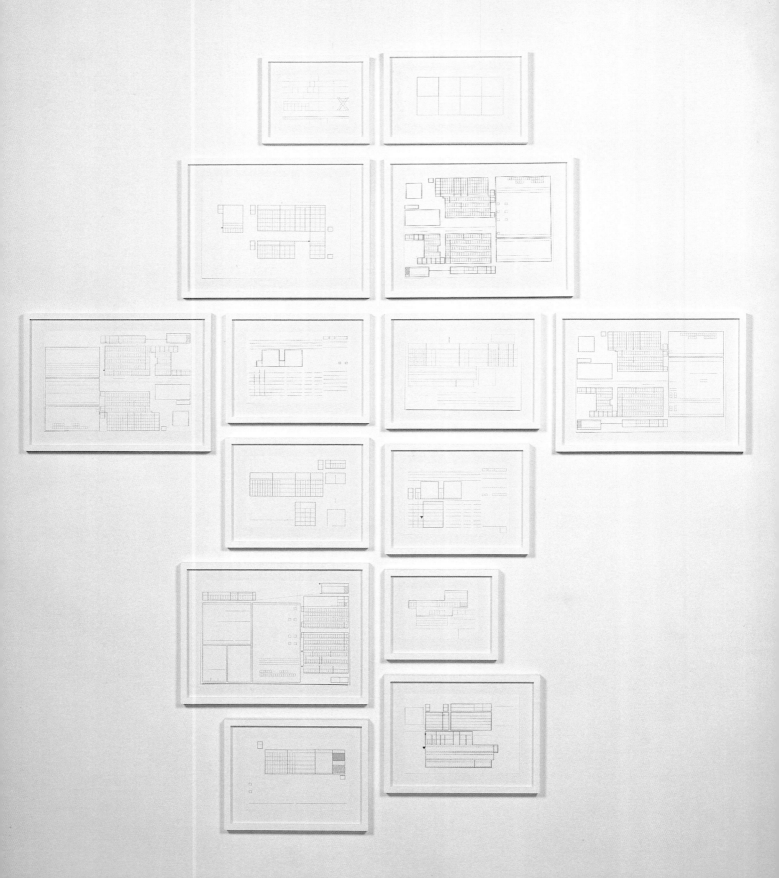

columns appear to float on a confidently brushed-in background. At a glance *From Nature* suggests spontaneity and ease of facture but closer study reveals something odd about the relationship between figure and ground. It is spatially puzzling, not least because the ground stands proud of the figure. And if it is a 'nature' painting, what are its sources? Here is Richard Hamilton reflecting on his return to nature – in his case to landscape painting – in the 1950s. It 'came second-hand through the use of magazines.... Somehow it didn't seem necessary to hold onto that older tradition of direct contact with the world'.[6] In *From Nature* Parsons is in fact using 'a fortuitous source' – a found scrap of paper on which a signature has been practised four times. This image has been enlarged and turned on its side. It has been copied with extreme care, its forms masked while the 'ground' was applied, the masking removed and the image thinly painted in. The status of *From Nature* is, therefore, complicated. It is a display of an existing source, an image mediated by an unknown hand and, at first misleading sight, a gestural painting. If the viewer knew nothing of *From Nature*'s genesis would it matter? Yes and no. By any standard it is a grand and mysterious work. As Parsons fully understands 'the experience is the important thing'. In art it is only results that count. But Parsons' interest in visual representation works within a continuum, a rather more demanding history of art than the evolutionary model.

6 Richard Hamilton,
Collected Words 1953–1982,
Thames and Hudson, n.d., p.64.

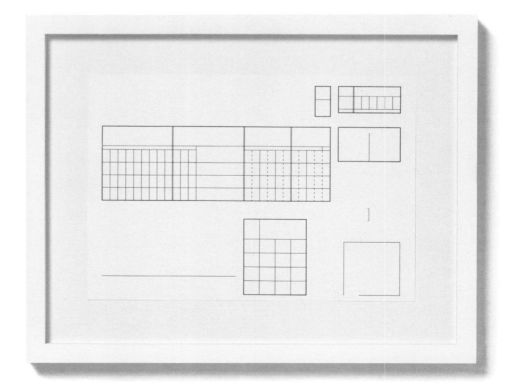

Architectural Form iv 1997
Laser xerograph on paper,
edition of ten
147 x 210 mm (5¾ x 8¼ in)

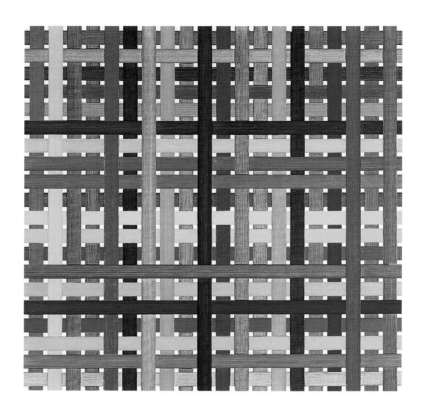

World View (Diastereomer) 1:2 1999
Oil on canvas
665 x 665 mm (26 x 26 in)

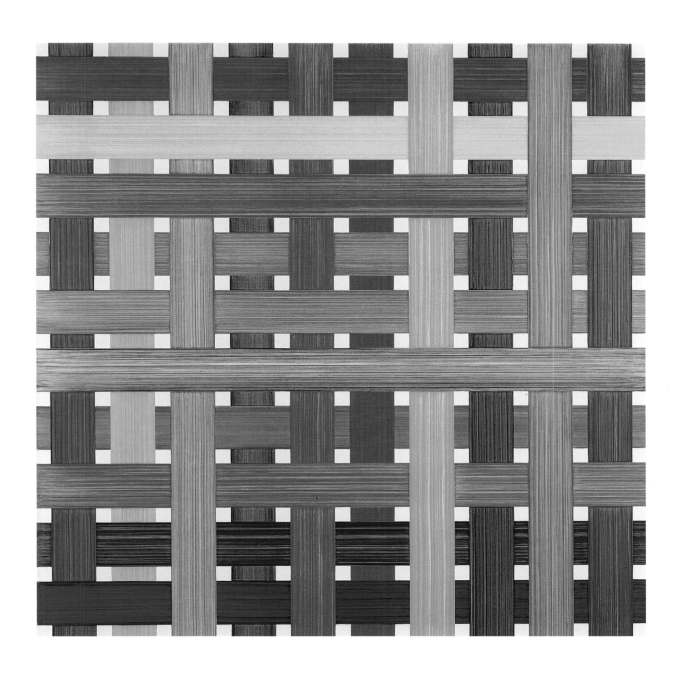

Formulation Picture (Space Lattice) 2000
Oil on canvas
1225 x 1225 mm (48 x 48 in)

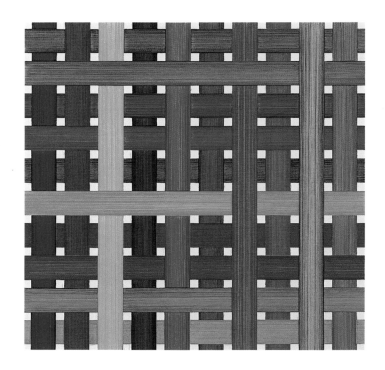

Aspect (Space Lattice) 2000
Oil on canvas
613 x 613 mm (24 x 24 in)

The artists in whom Parsons takes an interest are painters after his own heart. They tend to be investigative both as regards technique (Brice Marden's use of mark making devices which extend the brush) and in their attitude to canonical art (Gerhard Richter's meditations on composition and abstraction). In particular, Parsons admires the work of Jasper Johns. This is of interest because Jasper Johns' early paintings seemed to reify a body of theoretical writing. In retrospect, the synchronicity of Jasper Johns' art of the 1950s (the flag paintings) and Roland Barthes' writing of the same period (in particular an essay on the semiotics of a *Paris-Match* photograph of a black French soldier saluting the tricolour) is remarkable – it seems unlikely that Johns read Barthes at that early date.

Parsons, on the other hand, inhabits a more highly theorised world. The links between his art and theoretical discourse – particularly that of semiotics – are more marked and less accidental, but they relate to Johns' oeuvre. For instance Parsons' own uses of maps and flags carry forward Johns' intuitive understanding of the way in which such objects function as powerful signs. I am stressing Parsons' activity as a painter, but his series of dissected maps displayed in vitrines are amongst his most haunting works.[7] They are matched by his work with flags. Parsons makes alterations to the colours of extant flags, demonstrating how as viewers we frequently fail to recognise anomalous versions of familiar objects. With alarming ease we automatically see what we think we already know. But what might seem simply to be an example of perceptual laziness is given a twist by Parsons' choice of emblems of nationhood and national identity.

Parsons' remarkable grid paintings similarly conjoin with a body of theoretical writing. In particular they are given a context by Rosalind Krauss' meditations on the genre, especially her observations on the ways in which the form fulfils the expectations of intuitive and empirical artists alike. Parsons clearly finds this dualism liberating. Thus the titles of Parsons' grids – such as *World View (Diastereomer) 1:2* – suggest they belong to both the worlds of poetry and science. And Parsons is keenly aware of the poetic dimension of empirical sciences like organic chemistry. As he points out, in order to understand the structure of molecules scientists need to make their theories visually manifest. To do this they construct three dimensional models. These unexpectedly playful objects are the 'best possible model of reality they can come up with'.

Parsons too is working on the best possible model of reality he can come up with. Majestic paintings like *Man* and the watercolour diptych *The Character of Human Impulsion* embody the trials and beauties of that quest. So too do a series of much smaller works on paper that faithfully transcribe graffiti chalk marks. They belong to a family of 'basic scribbles' identified by American educationalist Rhoda Kellogg – twenty markings made universally by very

7 On maps see Robert Harbison, *Eccentric Spaces*, Secker and Warburg, 1989, pp.124 and 134. On the conceptual quality of maps – 'we find this pure conceptuality an illusion if we turn one upside down, so to see a familiar map with north at the bottom shows us how much it has become a picture' and 'Maps are both word and image too, both more synthetic and more abstract, higher and emptier than most literature or painting'.

15

young children. They are, therefore, acultural and form the building blocks of visual representation. *Tail*, *Opening* and *Coupling* are all simulacra of these haunting Ur-marks using the reverse technique Parsons employs for *From Nature* and *Man*, in which the ground in effect defines the figure. It is, incidentally, hard to find an appropriate vocabulary to convey Parsons' recreation of his various source materials. To understand his processes fully a Ruskinian sensitivity to the exigencies of the copy is required. For John Ruskin and for many Victorians the 'copy' was more than simply a mapping of a work of art. Rather it was a meditative performance, an act of creativity which set out to create a system of valued objects.

I hope that I have indicated something of the complexity of Parsons' art and suggested something of its meticulous beauty. Although Parsons works in many media, always creating the appropriate mode of production for the ideas he wishes to convey, his oeuvre has a remarkable unity. Which brings me finally to the late Alfred Gell's *Art and Agency: An Anthropological Theory*. It is a fiendishly difficult book but, as with the Jasper Johns/Roland Barthes relationship, there appears to be a coincidental synchronicity between Gell's thinking and Parsons' art. At the end of *Art and Agency* Gell argues for viewing an artist's oeuvre as a 'distributed object' – by which he means that artworks should not be seen as singular entities but rather as ensembles:

> each separate work is a modification, a recension, of previous ones, the leftovers of a particular cycle in a career-long generate-and-test sequence. To be sure, this model is somewhat idealised, and much of art consists of routine output rather than the results of strivings after perfection. But the more inventive and historically important artists do develop in this way, and their work can be read as a cumulative process of discovery.[8]

Gell viewed semiotics as useless to the interpretation of art objects and for that reason *Art and Agency* might seem a perverse concluding text. But Gell's vision of art as a system of action, in which art has no intrinsic nature, opens new doors for a generalised understanding both of the extraordinary, demanding work of Jonathan Parsons and of the character of ambitious art in our time.

8   Alfred Gell, *Art and Agency: An Anthropological Theory*, Oxford 1998, p.237.

Tanya Harrod

Extracts from a conversation between
Jonathan Parsons and Christine Kapteijn

CK *Your work is very diverse: you use different media and techniques. You create sculpture as well as paintings and drawings. In terms of technique there is an even greater diversity: watercolour, textiles, oil, ink, chalk. What links these different ways of working?*

JP I think the most important thing is for the particular method of production to be the most appropriate for any given concept.

CK *How do you decide?*

JP Well it's almost dictated by the source material or what I'm thinking about at the time. So, for example, for the the ink on paper drawing, *Skeleton,* the properties of the medium that are essential to its production are that it is capable of drawing a very long continuous line that smoothly and accurately records the tremor of the hand, because that was the kind of image I was wanting to create. Naturally, the medium had to be a technical ink pen on smooth paper.

CK *So it's not the source material of the flag which dictates the technique?*

JP No, no I am not just talking about the material, it's also whatever the idea is.

CK *I'm just intrigued that you mention first the image you wanted to create as dictating the medium, and not the textile nature of the flag in* Skeleton.

JP The tremor of the hand gives that textile effect, and it was important to find a medium which could record that. It would have been impossible to make it an oil painting. So the diversity of the appearance of the work in a sense belies the true nature of the investigation, because obviously an ink drawing is going to look different from an oil painting. The matter of finding the most appropriate technique is crucial to the way I go about deciding on how to produce work.

What I wanted to recreate in *The Character of Human Impulsion,* for example, was the subtlety of the dripping paint. It just seemed to me that watercolour was the appropriate medium to do that with. It's always a question of the most appropriate artistic materials for the given concept and source.

Coupling 2000
Pastel on paper
157 x 759 mm (6¼ x 29¾ in)

Opening 1999
Graphite on blue paper
150 x 470 mm (6 x 18½ in)

CK *Yes, it seems to me that Chomsky says that verbal language results from the interplay of essentially given structures of mind, developing as a result of interaction with the environment. And I think that you can also apply that to the experience of the visual arts. Now I'm not sure that you can apply that to the creation of it, in a sense I don't know how you would relate to that as an artist.*

JP Yes, well, in terms of subject matter I would certainly be interested in this kind of developmental idea, that there are certain innate structuring traits of brain function, that then produce phenomena which have some sort of resonance no matter from which culture they come.

CK *I see it in* Babies Blue *for instance, where I think that if you are talking about cultural logos, the flag as a national logo...*

JP As a representational token of collective self-identity. I don't really like the word logo.

CK *Well you mentioned it yourself in your concerns...*

JP What I was saying was that the flag has almost become like a logo these days, because it's used on packaging; it's used on products, as if it is a logo. When, in fact, it is a more complicated representational token. But I find it very interesting that you make that connection with the flags in terms of the multicultural connections between these kind of fundamental ideas. Because that is very much how I see the found gestural mark pieces (*Kiss*, *Tail*), as a kind of evidence for fundamental human characteristics, traces of these impulses, these innate drives as it were. I am certainly interested in trying to understand the constituents of such visual phenomena made by people. So when we were talking about Chomsky's desire to understand the operation of language, I'm interested in the materials of the human visual world. How images are made, why they are made, what they are made of and how devices of representation operate, the operational system.

CK *I also think, for instance, that a strategy which Chomsky devised for determining how language operates is disruption, and I think disruption in your work is also part of the visual process. For instance Chomsky mentions two sentences like 'John appealed to Bill to like himself', and 'John appeared to Bill to like himself'. With only one letter difference, the total meaning of that sentence changes, as a result of a small disruption.*

JP Well, my programme is certainly one of disruption of expectation. I would like to get in the way of what a viewer expects to see, and in some way thereby point out the strange nature of the structures we impose upon our perceptions.

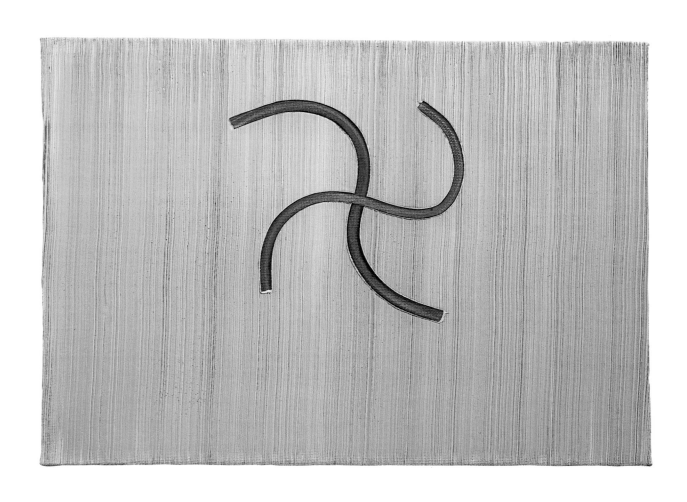

Masking Variation 9: Maligned Arrangement
1999
Oil on canvas
240 x 333 mm (9½ x 13 in)

CK *The strange nature of the process? Of viewing and presenting?*

JP And manipulating the environment …

CK *Is it more to do with what you are creating? Or is it also to do with what is received?*

JP I think it is both. In order to grasp or cope with the enormous complexity of the world, our brains filter out a lot. We encourage that, we are conditioned for that, by whichever culture we develop in. And so the artwork is a kind of catalyst for undermining that conditioning, pointing up the filters we have across our perceptions. To me, the artwork is the fundamental phenomenon around which openings up of our perceptions can revolve, so there is naturally an element of disruption in that kind of an idea, that the artwork can be a catalyst for expansion of awareness.

CK *Are you conscious of an audience?*

JP I think so, I think any artist who makes work and exhibits it, and then says they are only doing work for themselves is not being entirely truthful. If you only make work for yourself, it will be some sort of therapy and the work will be stored or destroyed afterwards. It wouldn't be exhibited and written about and photographed and sold on to collectors.

CK *It reminds me of discussions on the theme 'Does the artwork exist if it is never seen'.*

JP Well, I think that art as a manifestation doesn't exist outside its reception and the exhibition of art is the most concentrated arena for its reception. So I would say that in its most refined and powerful sense art doesn't exist outside exhibition and presentation.

CK *In what sense do you think interaction between the artwork and the viewer is of importance to the artist? Is it important to you?*

JP I think it is absolutely essential: the work isn't complete until it is received.

CK *I was going to talk about ambiguity. There's a sort of ambiguity in your work, but it seems to me to be controlled. Do you award this a special place in the experience of the visual arts?*

JP I think that ambiguity is a key quality of modern art, because there is no specific meaning or narrative or symbolic purpose behind a lot of modern art.

CK *Has there ever been a specific purpose?*

JP I don't know, I was trying to be accurate while generalising by saying

Man 1997
Oil on canvas
603 x 911 mm (23¾ x 36 in)

From Nature 1999
Oil on canvas
865 x 920 mm (34 x 36 in)

Whilst a Man is Free 1999
Oil on canvas
1727 x 1829 mm (68 x 72 in)

'modern art'. I have a feeling that ambiguity is pretty essential to all art, although if one thinks of altar pieces in specific churches made at a specific time, then these have a very specific purpose. They are designed to be understood in terms of the symbolism of the day, and in terms of the context in which they're displayed, and they're usually permanently displayed in that context.

CK *But you work with flags, also with very specific maps.*

JP Well, the sources are specific, the experiences of the sources are very particular to a certain culture, yes.

CK *Anybody can see that* Skeleton *is a flag, that's a start.*

JP The useful thing about a flag is that it is universal.

CK *Why the colour blue in* Babies Blue?

JP Well, the reason I use blue is simply because there are six blues available from traditional flag makers. I mean I'm also interested in working in fairly traditional forms, oil painting, water-colour, flag making, but of course using flag making as an art medium is a modern idea. It's part of a modern tradition of using other types of media for artwork. The flags themselves are made in an extremely traditional way. I was interested in working through the permutations of traditional ways of making. That's another thing I'm interested in; how do we relate traditional modes and practices to issues of contemporary relevance? The status of modern mimetic art, the status of representation, the status of the human body in non-mimetic art.

CK *How do you judge what is important to us in that context?*

JP Difficult to say. All I can say straight away is that the more I am involved in making, the more I become involved with thinking about ways of making, and therefore that kind of builds upon an interest that's already there, that augments it and consolidates it. The interest comes from the practice, I suppose.

CK *The more you do it the more you …*

JP Think about it and it leads you on to things that are connected with the practice.

CK *There's no over controlling world view at its basis? There is nothing that pervades all in your activities, a search for fundamentals perhaps?*

JP I guess it comes down to the fundamental questions about why we are

Cipher 2000
Oil on canvas
482 x 482 mm (19 x 19 in)

conscious of existing and how we deal with that self-consciousness: the significance of existence in the face of scientific discussions of the enormity of the cosmos, the fundamental insecurities of being a human.

CK *For instance, has* Carcass, *been reworked into* Study for a Crucifixion?

JP It is the same process, but a different map.

CK *Of the whole of Britain this time?*

JP Yes, the map used in *Carcass* crucially didn't have any references to Ireland in it. Or it may have had Northern Ireland floating on its own. I just forgot about all the islands, and strung up the mainland bit of Britain. With *Study for a Crucifixion* I had this map which also had, at the same scale, the entirety of the island of Ireland. So I thought I would retain that and also retain the other little islands as well, which you see there on the base of the case. I decided it would be more interesting to make the piece something which was specifically in the round, that didn't have a front or back, like *Carcass* seemed to have. It is much more explicitly three dimensional. And it just so happened that the two arms that support England, Scotland and Wales there, and the single arm that supported Ireland, when viewed from a particular alignment, suggested the form of a cross. I was already thinking about the representation of the human body, and about how the map dissections I did before had medical analogies, and referred to the body. And it just came together in the process of working out how to display the dissections and the idea of a dissected body, as it were. It just sort of suggested this theme of crucifixion.

CK *Is it the body of Christ?*

JP The interesting thing is, that this is where the viewers' own prejudices come in, if you like, that a crucifixion necessarily has to be Christ. But in fact people are still being crucified today. It's still a hideous method of execution. I also wanted to touch upon another innate drive of humanity, which seems to be violence. So with my very delicate, quiet and subtle works of art I just for a moment wanted to indicate something else a bit more difficult to deal with beyond the realm of how art is seen and made. Going back to *Babies Blue*, I have a feeling that these national flags, represented as they are, may point to a symbolism of the colour blue in connection with how that could be applied to specific regimes and constitutions.

CK *Of the industrialised world?*

JP Well, I think that we forget that right now the American and UK

Skeleton 1998
Indian ink on paper
2038 x 1120 mm
(80¼ x 44¼ in)

31

Skeleton 2000
Indian ink on paper
1372 x 1016 mm (54 x 40 in)

RIGHT
Skeleton 2000
detail

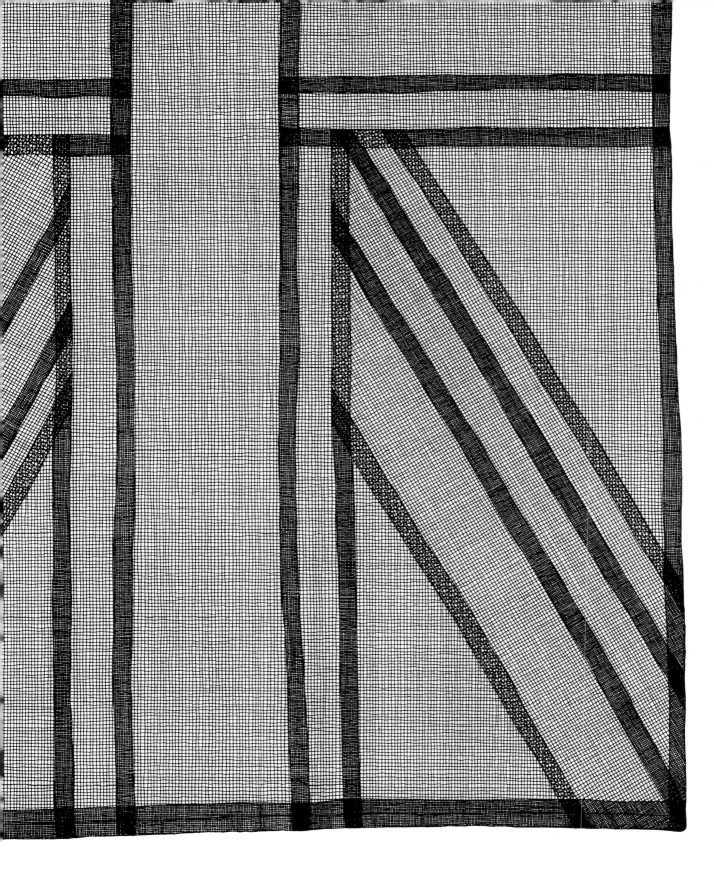

Commune 1998
31 sewn polyester flags with wall mounted flagstaffs
overall dimenions variable, each unit 990 x 950 x 75
mm (39 x 37½ x 3 in)

34

Babies Blue 2000
Eight sewn polyester flags with wall mounted flagstaffs
overall dimensions variable, each unit approximately
1880 x 1860 x 90 mm (74 x 73 x 3½ in)

35

governments are bombing Iraq every single day. And this kind of thing no one mentions. To me there is a sadness about that, that there is nothing we can do about it really.

CK *Can we not individually, can we not live differently?*

JP Yes, yes, but there is nothing much we can do to directly stop the bombs. I think that within whichever system, whatever you believe is right for a country, there is a kind of melancholy behind the whole engine of government. Maybe something like that lies behind *Babies Blue*.

CK *But you also talk of archetype and archaeology don't you?*

JP Artworks are what I call receptacles of the moment. They are of their time in a concentrated form. But I also think that they can refer to archetypes; they can refer to systems and structures outside the specifics of their own existence, of their own construction.

CK *Which are related to history, have been built up of histories?*

JP Absolutely, and some works are only that. Some works are only related to historical reference. And some works perhaps are only very transitory in nature and refer only to a very specific time and place. But I think that the works of art that persist, that have some sort of self-sufficiency are the ones that are indeed exactly of their own time, but also have qualities which can connect to other times, places. For me the idea of the art object as the receptacle of the moment is that it can be a repository for an idea which can project itself across time and space.

CK *Yes, because, for instance, the notion of the flag has changed, hasn't it?*

JP Absolutely, and we were talking about Dutch master paintings the other day, and the fact that we see them today in different terms from those in which they were seen originally. But we are still able to find in them very specific and interesting qualities.

CK *I think that what we were going to talk about was how you perceive yourself as part of a modernist tradition, weren't we?*

JP Oh yes, we were talking earlier about my interest in traditional forms and practices. I very much see myself located within the modernist tradition. And, for example, in *Skeleton* I wanted to relate that kind of minimalist grid appearance to a specific reference to cloth. I am shifting the intention and meaning behind the idea of a grid of ink lines from a purely minimalistic materialist motif, to a specifically representational device.

Brushstroke/Flag 1998
Indian ink on paper
218 x 290 mm (8½ x 11½ in)

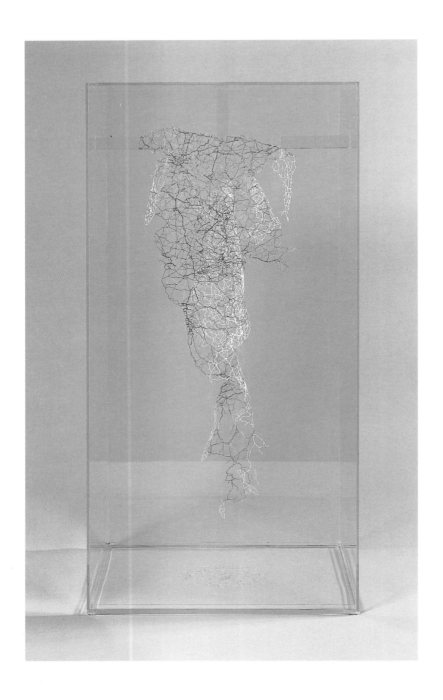

Study for a Crucifixion 2000
Dissected map in acrylic case
1200 x 600 x 600 mm (47¼ x 23¾ x 23¾ in)

Study for a Crucifixion 2000
detail

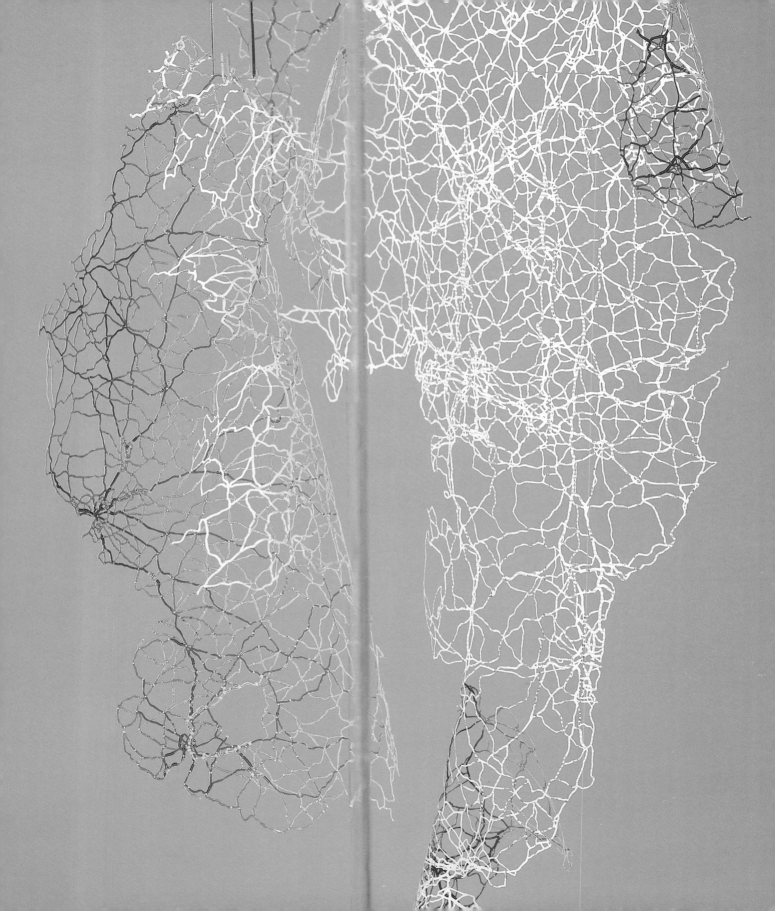

CK *It goes back to history then doesn't it, straight back to representation?*

JP Yes, absolutely, and I think that it is really crucial to what I do, this idea of how representations are made. The flag is a very useful object for me because it is a representational token that is in almost universal use and therefore it's a symptom of one of the fundamental drives of humanity, which is to make representations. And because it's unquestioned it becomes almost invisible. It only becomes visible when its codes are violated. By taking apart these forms of representation or tokens, I'm hoping again to demonstrate the strange nature of the structures imposed upon perception.

CK *But why return to representation? In fact, why progress towards representation?*

JP I just think it is a fundamental quality of human visual life, this urge for people to represent things, all over the place, everywhere. This thing of making one's mark, leaving some sort of tiny scrap of evidence that one existed in the world.

CK *Is it representation also, in contrast with abstraction?*

JP Yes it's overtly mimetic. Abstract is a word I don't really like because I think it is very confusing. A painting by Vermeer is abstract, for example, because it is a very specific conceptual and mechanical system. It's a very particular type of artificial image that is not necessarily the most realistic way of making a view of an interior.

CK *No, in that sense the terms are strange, aren't they? They themselves have undergone tremendous development according to our experience. It seems that our daily experience is becoming more and more abstract, so the terms themselves have shifted.*

JP Abstract, for me, means of the mind and earlier could have been equated with conceptual in a sense, so I think it is very confusing to talk about abstract paintings.

CK *Well conceptual is perhaps better then, but then you could say all art is conceptual, couldn't you?*

JP Exactly, it's too general. That's why I like the word mimetic, because that's very specifically something which apes the appearance of something else. And certainly *Skeleton* is mimetic, but it's an abstracted mimesis, if we can say that.

CK *Yes, in that sense it is very different from the minimalist abstractions, isn't it?*

JP Yes, the use of the minimalist grid was an almost arbitrary system of presenting the material qualities of the substances used in the construction.

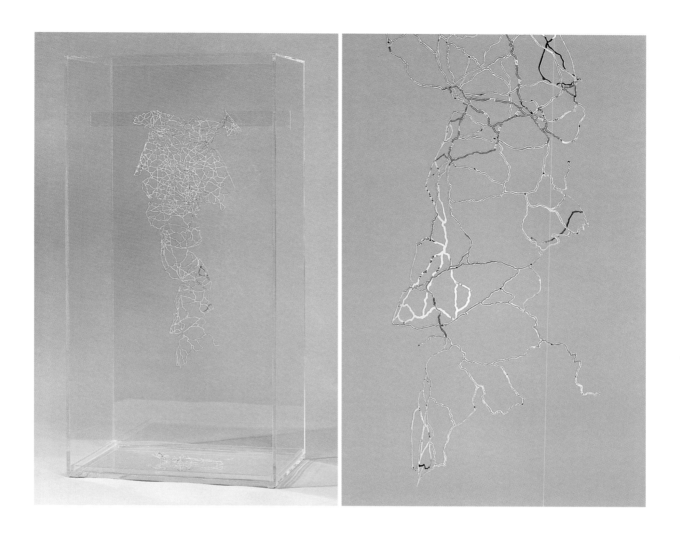

Small Study for a Crucifixion 2000
Dissected map in acrylic case
800 x 400 x 280 mm (31½ x 15¾ x 11 in)

Small Study for a Crucifixion 2000
detail

41

**The Character of
Human Impulsion** 2000
Watercolour on paper
diptych, each panel 1127 x 608 mm
(44½ x 24 in)

And I think the grid must have grown out of the rectangle, because we live in the culture of the rectangle. James Turrell said something very interesting about the rectangle being so widely used, because in Western architecture it is a neutral thing. If we lived in circular buildings, we may not have had the convention of rectangular easel paintings. And also flags point out this obsession with the rectangular format that we have in this culture.

CK *Yes, also it is the most efficient shape, isn't it, presumably in terms of space?*

JP In terms of Western architectural space, sure, but in terms of strength or structural stability the sphere is more efficient, so it depends in what terms you are talking about.

CK *It's interesting how you use mimetic, and that's such a classical Aristotelian word, isn't it, of imitating, following and then surpassing. So is for you standing on the shoulders of one's predecessors important?*

JP The most useful art for me to look at is art which is very ancient, beyond the cradle of civilisation. Its original function is so impossible for us to know that we are forced to look at it only in formal terms. And that art has this kind of archetypal quality; these works persist through historical good fortune, but also then have a sort of self-perpetuating quality, perhaps because they are robbed of their original context.

CK *Yes, perhaps because its appearance appeals to a universal sense?*

JP That's another thing, yes.

CK *A sense that is still with us, maybe rudimentary, but is still there. It may not be rational, of course, but it's intuitive.*

JP Absolutely, I was just thinking when we were talking about that of a remarkable painting in Australia, a painting on a rock wall, that's protected by a shelf, outside. It's supposed to be about 10,000 years old, a huge wall of multicoloured hand prints, all the earth colours you can think of: cream, brown, black, red, orange, yellow, blue occasionally. Apparently, they were the marks of every single person in that community who had ever lived. So they printed their hand onto this huge communal surface, and it's come down to us and survived and is stunning, an absolutely stunning painting. It's quite moving, incredible, and I think that the thing that's so moving about the rock paintings in Lascaux in France is the handprints, where they have put their hand out and used a mouthful of paint as an aerosol spray.

CK *Yes, and that still goes on, doesn't it?*

JP Mann's Chinese Theatre in Hollywood.

CK *That's definitely archetypal, the idea that your identity is a hand, a signature, is quite interesting isn't it? There must be something primeval in that.*

JP There is something about reaching out and touching, or just the fact that the hand is the thing with which we manipulate the environment. The first thing the child does is to reach out and touch. Well, this is what takes us back to what you were asking before, what is the fundamental reason for doing this, where do these interests come from. And one of these things is surely: the number of things in the universe is overwhelming if one tries to think about it.

CK *Do you think it's a spiritual awareness, consciousness?*

JP Yes, this idea about consciousness, the fact that to get a total grasp of any of these works is impossible. In fact, this reflects the condition of existence, which is never really knowing. Like the unknowable nature of God as described in many theologies.

CK *But we still have to work with it?*

JP We still have to cope. That's where some of these drives come from, coping with the enormity of knowing that we exist. I doubt that we can truly know that we exist, but we feel very strongly that we do. 'I think therefore I am', is a debatable proposition, but we can be generally sure that we exist.

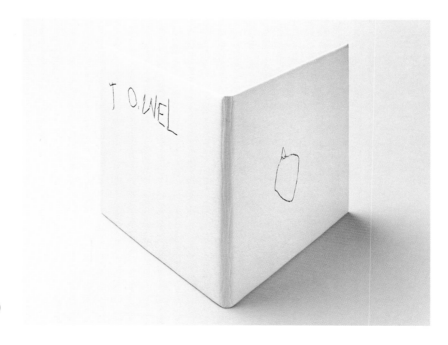

Towel 1998
Collaboration with
Tracey Rowledge
Alum-tawed goatskin tooled in
blue & black carbon with
alum-tawed calfskin doublures,
edition of five
100 x 150 x 8 mm (4 x 6 x ¼ in)
(closed)

JONATHAN PARSONS

Born 26 May 1970

Education

1989–1992
University of London Goldsmiths' College
BA Honours degree

1988–1989
West Surrey College of Art and Design
College diploma in foundation studies

Solo Exhibitions

1999–2000
Recent Work, Richard Salmon, London

1996
Richard Salmon, London

1994
Heber-Percy Gallery, Leamington Spa

Selected Group Exhibitions

2000
Drawing, Percy Miller Gallery, London
British Art Show 5, Hayward Gallery National Touring
 Exhibition for the Arts Council of England
The Art of Barbie, Proud Galleries, London
See For Yourself, Peterborough Museum and Art Gallery
Ripe, Crafts Council Gallery, London

1999
East Wing Collection, Courtauld Institute of Art, London
Sensation, Brooklyn Museum of Art, New York
Saatchi in Sheffield, Mappin Art Gallery, Sheffield
Furniture, John Hansard Gallery, Southampton

1998
Sensation, Hamburger Bahnhof, Berlin
Educating Barbie, Trans Hudson Gallery, New York
Anthem: Jonathan Parsons, Neil Goldberg, Milch, London
Craft, Aberystwyth Arts Centre
In a Meeting, Grayson House, London
Pictura Britannica: Art From Britain, Te Papa Museum,
 New Zealand

1997
Pictura Britannica: Art From Britain, Art Gallery
 of South Australia, Adelaide
Craft, Kettle's Yard, Cambridge
Light, Spacex Gallery, Exeter
Sensation, Royal Academy of Arts, London
Sequence, Richard Salmon, London
Pictura Britannica: Art From Britain, The Museum
 of Contemporary Art, Sydney
Plastic, Walsall Museum and Art Gallery
Building Site, Architectural Association, London

1996
Plastic, Arnolfini, Bristol

1994
The City of Dreadful Night, Atlantis Lower Gallery, London
Every Now and Then, Rear Window at
 Richard Salmon Ltd, London

1992
The Coventry Open, Herbert Art Gallery, Coventry

Public Collections

Arts Council Collection
UK Government Art Collection

Selected Press

Duncan Macmillan, 'Not So Subtle Wordplay', *The Scotsman*,
 12 April 2000
Robin Young & Jonathan Morgan, 'Broad canvas for new
 face of Tate Britain', *The Times*, 24 March 2000
Gaby Wood, 'This is British Art: The Work',
 Observer Magazine, 19 March 2000
Izi Glover, 'Jonathan Parsons', *Time Out*, 19–26 January 2000
Lisa Panting, 'Changing Topography', *Contemporary Visual
 Arts*, Issue 24 1999
Mark Currah, 'Neil Goldberg, Jonathan Parsons',
 Time Out, 2–9 September 1998
Louisa Buck, 'London Calling: Milch Moves South',
 The Art Newspaper No.83, July–August 1998
'The Hot 100' (& front cover image), *Sunday Times Magazine*,
 24 May 1998
Margot Coatts, 'Bound to Please', *Crafts*, March/April 1998

John Windsor, 'Let The Love Affair Begin', *Independent Saturday Magazine*, 17 January 1998

Maria Alvarez, 'Red, White and Cool', *Telegraph Magazine*, 8 November 1997

Courtney Kidd, 'Pictura Britannica', *Art Monthly*, November 1997

Richard Dorment, 'Sensation? What Sensation?', *The Daily Telegraph*, 17 September 1997

Elaine Paterson, 'Arts About Face', *Time Out*, 10–17 September 1997

Robert Garnett, 'Plastic', *Art Monthly*, October 1996

'Critic's Choice', *Time Out*, 17–24 July 1996

Sacha Craddock, 'Around the Galleries', *The Times*, 16 July 1996

Iain Gale, 'There Are More Ways of Seeing', *The Independent*, 16 July 1996

'Jonathan Parsons', *The Week*, 13 July 1996

Mark Currah, 'Jonathan Parsons', *Time Out*, 10–17 July 1996

'Critic's Choice', *Time Out*, 10–17 July 1996

Pick of the Week, 'Jonathan Parsons', *The Independent*, 2 July 1996

Rob Kesseler, 'The City of Dreadful Night', *Untitled*, Spring 1995

Tania Guha, 'The City of Dreadful Night', *Time Out*, 7–14 December 1994

Sacha Craddock, 'Around The Galleries', *The Times*, 29 November 1994

Gareth Jones, 'Every Now and Then', *Flash Art*, October 1994

Mark Currah, 'Every Now and Then', *Frieze*, June–August 1994

Mark Currah, 'Every Now and Then', *Time Out*, 11–18 May 1994

William Harvey, 'Every Now and Then', *Untitled*, Summer 1994

Books & Catalogues

Judith Bumpus, Pippa Coles, Matthew Higgs, Tony Godfrey, Jacqui Poncelet
British Art Show 5
Hayward Gallery, London 2000

The Art of Barbie
Vision On Publishing, London 2000

Louise Taylor, et al.
Ripe
Crafts Council, London 2000

Isobel Johnstone, et al.
The Saatchi Gift to the Arts Council Collection
Hayward Gallery Publishing, London 1999

Jonathan Barnbrook, ed.
Young British Art: the Saatchi Decade
Booth-Clibborn Editions, London 1998

David Burrows, Mark Harris, Peter Lloyd Lewis
Educating Barbie
Trans Hudson Gallery, New York 1998

Simon Watney, Janis Jefferies, Roy Voss, Joan Key
Craft
Richard Salmon, London; Kettle's Yard, Cambridge 1997

Norman Rosenthal, et al.
Sensation
Royal Academy of Arts; Thames and Hudson, London 1997

Bernice Murphy, ed.
Pictura Britannica
The Museum of Contemporary Art, Sydney 1997

Neil Cummings, Paul Heber-Percy, Joan Key
Plastic
Richard Salmon, London; Arnolfini, Bristol 1996

Rear Window
Mirror Mirror
Rear Window Publications, London 1996

Richard Salmon, et al.
Jonathan Parsons
Richard Salmon, London 1996

Published to accompany the exhibition Jonathan Parsons: System + Structure.
Produced by the James Hockey Gallery, The Surrey Institute of Art & Design,
University College, Farnham Campus, Falkner Road, Farnham, Surrey GU9 7DS

Curated by Christine Kapteijn

Exhibition Venues
James Hockey Gallery   23 October – 9 December 2000
Stanley Picker Gallery   12 April – 19 May 2001
The Lowry   8 September – 28 October 2001

ISBN 1 899817 05 0

Designed by Ray Carpenter
Typeset by Tom Knott
Printed by Richard Edward Ltd

Photographic Credits
Page 1, Photography by the artist.
Page 45, Photography by Lesley Davies-Evans. Photograph courtesy
Crafts Council. Reproduced by kind permission.
Page 13, © Crown copyright: UK Government Art Collection.
Photograph reproduced by kind permission.
All other photography by Stephen James of Prudence Cuming Associates Ltd.
Photographs, Pages 7–9, 12, 21, 25, 27, 31 and 48, courtesy Richard Salmon.

Funded by The Arts Council of England and South East Arts

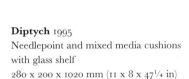

Diptych 1995
Needlepoint and mixed media cushions
with glass shelf
280 x 200 x 1020 mm (11 x 8 x 47¼ in)